ANIMALS ON THE BRINK

Grizzly Bears

Karen Dudley

www.av2books.com

AV² provides enriched content that supplements and complements this book. Weigl's AV² books strive to create inspired learning and engage young minds in a total learning experience.

Your AV² Media Enhanced books come alive with...

Audio
Listen to sections of the book read aloud.

Key Words
Study vocabulary, and complete a matching word activity.

Video
Watch informative video clips.

Quizzes
Test your knowledge.

Go to **www.av2books.com**, and enter this book's unique code.

BOOK CODE

R76705

Embedded Weblinks
Gain additional information for research.

Slide Show
View images and captions, and prepare a presentation.

AV² by Weigl brings you media enhanced books that support active learning.

Try This!
Complete activities and hands-on experiments.

... and much, much more!

Published by AV² by Weigl
350 5th Avenue, 59th Floor
New York, NY 10118
Websites: www.av2books.com   www.weigl.com

Library of Congress Control Number: 2013953039

ISBN 978-1-4896-0568-9 (hardcover)
ISBN 978-1-4896-0569-6 (softcover)
ISBN 978-1-4896-0570-2 (single-user eBook)
ISBN 978-1-4896-0571-9 (multi-user eBook)

Printed in the United States of America in North Mankato, Minnesota
1 2 3 4 5 6 7 8 9   17 16 15 14 13

122013
WEP301113

Project Coordinator Aaron Carr
Design Mandy Christiansen

Every reasonable effort has been made to trace ownership and to obtain permission to reprint copyright material. The publishers would be pleased to have any errors or omissions brought to their attention so that they may be corrected in subsequent printings.

Photo Credits
Weigl acknowledges Getty Images as its primary photo supplier for this title.

Contents

Take a Stand
·Debate·
·Research·

The Grizzly Bear

Grizzlies are sometimes thought of as vicious animals that attack humans for no reason. Even the name "grizzly bear" suggests a ferocious, fearsome beast. In reality, grizzly bears use their strength, teeth, and claws to defend themselves and to get food. They prefer to stay as far away from humans as possible.

This book will show you where the grizzly bear lives, what it eats, and how it spends its winters. You will also read about grizzly cubs and how they survive their first years of life. Find out why the grizzly is in danger of disappearing from parts of the United States and Canada, and learn what you can do to help.

There are many legends and stories about the grizzly bear. Folklore commonly describes the grizzly as a powerful animal that people both fear and admire. This book takes a close look at the grizzly bear in its natural **habitat** and will help you decide how you feel about the grizzly.

The average life span of a grizzly bear in nature is 25 years. Grizzlies in captivity have lived for more than 40 years.

How to Take a Stand on an Issue

Research is important to the study of any scientific field. When scientists choose a subject to study, they must conduct research to ensure they have a thorough understanding of the topic. They ask questions about the subject and then search for answers. Sometimes, however, there is no clear answer to a question. In these cases, scientists must use the information they have to form a hypothesis, or theory. They must take a stand on one side of an issue or the other. Follow the process below for each Take a Stand section in this book to determine where you stand on these issues.

1. **What is the Issue?**
   a. Determine a research subject, and form a general question about the subject.

2. **Form a Hypothesis**
   a. Search at the library and online for sources of information on the subject.
   b. Conduct basic research on the subject to narrow down the general question.
   c. Form a hypothesis on the subject based on research to this point.
   d. Make predictions based on the hypothesis. What are the expected results?

3. **Research the Issue**
   a. Conduct extensive research using a variety of sources, including books, scientific journals, and reliable websites.
   b. Collect data on the issue and take notes on all information gathered from research.
   c. Draw conclusions based on the information collected.

4. **Conclusion**
   a. Explain the research findings.
   b. Was the hypothesis proved or disproved?

Grizzlies are sometimes called "silvertips" because their fur can look white or silver in the sunshine.

Guide to the
Grizzly

Despite their size, grizzlies can walk silently through a forest.

Grizzlies spend more time digging than most other types of bears. Strong shoulder muscles give them extra power for digging.

Features

Grizzly bears are larger than most of the other animals in their habitat. They can weigh more than six adult humans, and they have long claws at the ends of large, strong paws. At a quick glance, a grizzly may easily be mistaken for another type of bear, such as the black bear. However, there are ways to distinguish grizzlies from black bears. The grizzly's large shoulder hump, made of fat and muscle, is one of the easiest ways to tell a grizzly bear from a black bear. Grizzlies also have shorter, rounder ears and longer claws that are lighter in color.

Grizzly bears are well adapted for their sometimes harsh environment. They are able to survive cold winters, eat many types of food depending on what is available, and defend themselves against the other animals that share their territory. These special features give grizzlies their nickname, "King of the Wilderness."

Grizzly bears vary greatly in size, depending on the bear's age, where it lives, and whether it is male or female. Adult male grizzly bears can weigh from 300 to more than 800 pounds (135 to 365 kilograms), and they can be 6 to 7 feet (1.8 to 2.1 meters) long from head to tail. Female grizzlies are 40 percent smaller than male grizzlies. They weigh about 200 to 500 pounds (90 to 225 kg) when full-grown. Grizzlies that live in areas where there is plenty of high-protein food, such as salmon, are often much larger than bears that eat mainly leaves, grasses, roots, and berries.

All grizzly bears are at their largest and fattest in late summer and early fall. At this time, the bears eat enormous amounts of food in preparation for winter. Over the winter, female grizzlies with cubs may lose 30 percent or more of their body weight.

From an Expert

"To see a wild bear is always exciting. No other animal so powerfully evokes the North American wilderness."
John A. Murray

John A. Murray is a naturalist who researched and photographed grizzly bears for many years. His books on grizzlies include *Grizzly Bears: An Illustrated Field Guide* and *The Great Bear: Contemporary Writings on the Grizzly*.

Classification

Bears are in the large **order** of animals that are **carnivores** and the smaller group, or family, that includes all bears. Scientists use the Latin names Carnivora and Ursidae for these groups. There are eight different **species** of bears in the world, including brown bears. The grizzly is a type, or subspecies, of brown bear.

Every known species and subspecies of animal is given a Latin name to describe it. This allows scientists from all over the world to understand exactly which animal is being discussed. A third word follows to describe each subspecies. The brown bear is *Ursus arctos*, and the grizzly bear is *Ursus arctos horribilis*.

Despite their differences, all bears share many similarities. They all have large heavy bodies, short tails, thick fur, large heads, and rounded ears. All bears walk on flat feet, and they have a good sense of smell. They all spend a great deal of time alone.

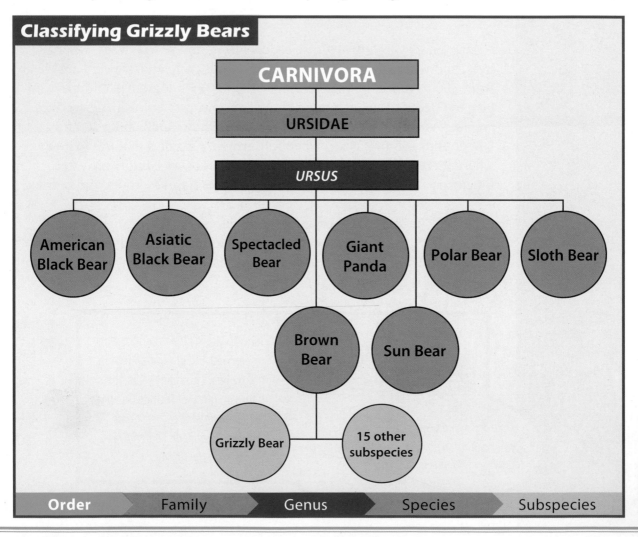

The American black bear is found in many parts of the United States and Canada. Black bears are smaller than grizzlies, but they have taller ears.

The grizzly is just one of the many types of brown bears found in North America, Europe, and Asia.

The sun bear, found in Southeast Asia, is the smallest of all bears.

Guide to the Grizzly

A grizzly's paws help the bear to cool off in hot weather. The ground is often cooler than the air. By resting their large paws on the ground, grizzlies help cool the rest of their bodies.

A grizzly's fur can change color from year to year.

Fur

Although grizzly bears are a type of brown bear, their fur can vary in color. Some grizzlies have fur that is off-white, and others are almost black. The fur of a brown-colored grizzly is often different shades of brown on different parts of its body. Some grizzly bears have fur with white or silver tips on the ends, which gives them a **grizzled** appearance. This is how the grizzly bear got its name.

The grizzly bear has two types of fur. The underfur is made up of short, soft, fine hair that is close to the bear's skin. The **guard hairs** are what we see when we look at a bear. They are longer and coarser than the underfur.

The two layers of fur work well together. They insulate the grizzly from the heat and the cold. They also protect the bear's skin from insects and dirt. A grizzly's fur helps to **camouflage** the bear in its natural habitat, and it is sometimes used as a form of communication. For example, an angry bear may raise the fur on its shoulders to appear more threatening.

Grizzlies molt once a year, during late spring and early summer. This means that they shed their thick outer fur. During molting, grizzlies rub against trees and rocks to help remove the old hair. When the bears are molting, they look very ragged.

Molting takes only a few weeks, and after molting, the grizzly bear has a shiny, sleek coat of fur. When colder weather approaches, grizzlies grow a thick new coat of longer fur to prepare them for winter.

The grizzly bear's fur can make it difficult to see the animal from a distance.

Guide to the
Grizzly

Before they enter their winter dens, grizzlies have often eaten so much that they have a layer of fat several inches thick.

Male grizzlies leave their dens earlier than females.

The Den

A den is a small enclosed area where a grizzly spends the winter. Most grizzlies dig their dens, often on a hillside or on the bank of a lake or river. Adult grizzlies almost always go into a den alone, although mothers will share a den with their cubs. Young grizzlies that have recently left their mothers will sometimes share a den with their siblings.

A grizzly's den is not much bigger than the bear itself. Once inside the den, the grizzly bear has only enough room to stretch and turn around. This helps the bear stay warm. The grizzly bear's body heat keeps the den warm all winter.

Grizzly dens are often covered by thick layers of snow during the winter. The snow helps to insulate the den from cold outside air and keep the bear warm. There is always an air passage to the outside of the den. This means that the bear can have fresh air all winter. Grizzly dens are often on steep slopes, so that melting snow and rain will easily drain away from the den opening. The entrance to the den is usually sheltered from strong winds.

It takes grizzly bears a few weeks to fully recover from their time in the den. Their first task after leaving the den is to find food. They move slowly at first, and they often must travel long distances to find green grass and other food to eat.

Grizzlies usually dig new dens every year, but they will sometimes return to a den they have used in the past.

Special Adaptations

Grizzly bears have many **adaptations**. These features help them survive the challenges of their environment.

Ears

Grizzlies have excellent hearing. Scientists believe that grizzly bears can hear the movements of ground squirrels underneath several inches (centimeters) of soil.

Eyes

For many years, people believed that grizzly bears had poor eyesight. Evidence now shows that their vision is as good as human eyesight. Grizzlies have color vision, which helps them find some of their favorite foods, such as ripe berries.

Teeth

Grizzly bears have 42 teeth and very powerful jaws. Along with its paws and claws, a grizzly's teeth are its main tools for defense and for obtaining food. Grizzly bears have long, sharp canine teeth in the fronts of their mouths for tearing and eating meat. They also have flat molar teeth that are used for grinding and chewing plant food.

Nose

Many scientists think that grizzlies have a better sense of smell than any other North American animal. It is their most important sense. Grizzlies can smell food sources that are several miles (kilometers) away. They also use their sense of smell to locate mates during mating season, to identify cubs, and to avoid humans.

Shoulders

The "hump" on the back of a grizzly bear is made of fat and very strong muscles. With these strong shoulder muscles, a grizzly can knock down a moose or an elk with just one swipe of a paw.

Paws

A grizzly bear uses its paws for walking, swimming, attacking prey, feeding, lifting, pulling, turning, and self-defense. A grizzly's paws look very big and awkward, but they are actually able to gently hold and move small objects, such as stones and berry branches.

Claws

At the end of each paw are five toes with nonretractable claws. This means the claws are fixed in an outstretched position and cannot be pulled in like the claws of a cat. A grizzly's claws grow to be as long as 6 inches (15 cm). The claws are used for digging dens, finding food, and scratching trees to mark the grizzly's territory.

Guide to the
Grizzly

With their excellent sense of smell, grizzlies can smell certain roots that are buried under several inches of soil, or even a stick of chewing gum that is in the glove compartment of an automobile.

A group of bears in one place almost always means that there is a great deal of food around.

Groups

Some animals must communicate constantly with one another, such as wolves living in packs. In contrast, grizzly bears spend most of their time alone. They avoid other bears, and they approach other animals only when hunting for food. Grizzlies need to spend so much of their time eating that they will avoid almost any situation that does not lead to a meal. Generally peaceful animals, bears usually choose easy meals over food that is difficult to obtain or that involves conflict. Grizzlies do not usually spend time fighting when they could be eating instead.

Although it is uncommon to see grizzly bears in groups, a group of bears is called a sloth. There are only a few times when a grizzly bear will accept the presence of another bear. During mating season in the spring, male and female grizzly bears will spend one or two weeks together. Grizzly cubs will spend their first few years with their mother. After leaving their mother, older cubs often spend their first season together before they each find new homes.

Grizzlies will also gather to feast at very good food sources. Bears that live near the coast will eat large amounts of salmon during the summer. From June to October, salmon leave the ocean and swim upstream in rivers to lay their eggs. There are so many salmon at this time that grizzly bears will stay near rivers and eat as much as possible. During the salmon season, as many as 15 grizzly bears have been seen fishing in one area of a river. There is so much salmon that grizzlies do not have to compete for food, so they accept the presence of other grizzlies.

Grizzlies are generally very quiet animals. However, they will grunt, snort, growl, and even roar to make their presence known. Young bear cubs will whine and squeal to communicate with their mother. Grizzlies also use markings to let other animals know they are in an area. A grizzly leaves its scent in an area by rubbing its body against the ground, a tree, or a rock. Grizzlies also mark an area when they urinate, leave behind droppings, or scratch the bark off tall trees.

Markings are most often left by male grizzlies.

Body Language

In addition to markings and sounds, grizzlies communicate through body language. Much of their body language is meant to help avoid conflict with other bears. If they are angry or uncomfortable, grizzlies may open their mouths, lower their heads, raise their noses, or flatten their ears. If two bears see one another in the distance, they communicate through their actions. The smaller of the two bears usually runs away from the larger.

Bluffing

A threatened grizzly will stare at an intruder or will "bluff." This means it will charge as if it is going to attack, only to stop and turn away before reaching the intruder. The bear may also slap its paws on the ground, blow air through its nose loudly, and make clacking sounds with its teeth. Grizzlies avoid fighting whenever possible and will usually try several types of bluffs first. However, a bear that has its ears pinned back may be finished bluffing. The bear may be preparing to attack.

Affection

Female grizzlies generally do not choose to interact with males unless they are ready to mate. Once a mating pair is matched up, they may show affection by chewing on each other's heads and necks. They play fight and nuzzle each other. The pair may also spend several days walking closely together.

Protection

Grizzly mothers will often stand on their hind legs to look out for danger when their cubs are nearby. She may warn an intruder to stay away by simply turning her body sideways. If she thinks her cubs are threatened by a human or another animal, she may charge at the threat or even attack. It is rare for a threatened grizzly mother to turn and run away.

Submission

If two male grizzlies are almost the same size, they will slowly approach each other and circle around until they decide who is bigger. Often, one bear will show that he is submissive or weaker by giving up and running away. A grizzly may also show that it is submissive by avoiding eye contact and sitting down or by yawning.

Should people be allowed to hunt grizzly bears?

In a few parts of Alaska and Canada, it is legal to hunt grizzly bears with a license from the government. Some people believe that hunting grizzlies is a way to keep bear populations from getting too large. Others believe that hunting threatens the grizzly's survival.

FOR

1. Hunting is limited, and only a few bears are taken each year. When there are many bears in an area, hunting some grizzlies can benefit other bears by allowing them more space and food.
2. The money made from selling hunting licenses can be spent on programs to study and protect the remaining bears. The money spent by hunters in an area also benefits local people.

AGAINST

1. Hunters sometimes sell the body parts of grizzly bears that are legally hunted. This may increase the demand for these items, which may increase **poaching**.
2. Humans should not kill any animals in nature. Grizzlies have a right to live peacefully in their habitat.

Mating and Birth

Grizzly bears usually mate in late spring or early summer, but their cubs are not born until the following January. Although there are many months between mating and the birth of the cubs, the **gestation period** of a female grizzly is only about three months. The reason for the difference in time is a process called delayed implantation. This means that a female grizzly's pregnancy will not start until the mother has eaten enough food in late summer and early autumn. In the months before entering her den, a female grizzly may gain as much as 3 pounds (1.3 kg) a day. Only a well-fed grizzly bear has enough fat to provide the warmth and nourishment that she and her cubs will need in the winter months. Delayed implantation is important to the survival of grizzly bears. It allows only the healthiest females to give birth to healthy cubs. It also means that in the fall, when there is a great deal of food available, the bears can focus on eating rather than mating.

A female grizzly bear usually gives birth to two cubs. However, she may have only one cub or, more rarely, up to four cubs. At birth, grizzly bear cubs are tiny, blind, and completely helpless. They are less than 1 foot (0.3 m) long from the tips of their noses to the ends of their tails. They weigh less than 1 pound (0.4 kg). Their eyes are closed, and they do not have any teeth. They are covered with very fine, pale hair, but they look as if they are completely bald. Newborn cubs gain weight quickly and need to nurse every two or three hours.

Newborn grizzly cubs will huddle together to keep warm until their fur gets longer and thicker.

Guide to the
Grizzly

Cubs gain hundreds of pounds in their first few years of life.

If an adult male and female grizzly are seen together, they are probably a mating pair.

Guide to the Grizzly

Although adult grizzlies rarely climb trees, cubs are very good climbers. They climb trees both in play and when their mother warns them of danger.

A grizzly mother may sit up or lie down while she is nursing her cubs. Sitting makes it easier for her to look out for danger.

Cubs

Grizzly cubs are raised entirely by their mother. In their first months in the den, the cubs rely on their mother for warmth and food. The mother's milk is very high in fat and protein. It provides the cubs with all the nutrients they need to survive. By late April to late May, if the weather has warmed up enough, the grizzly mother and her cubs leave the den to search for fresh food.

The family remains near the den until the cubs are older and stronger. The cubs gain strength by playing and exploring near their den. This prepares them for the long journeys they will make with their mother while she looks for food.

Cubs stay very close to their mother. By watching and imitating her, they learn how to find food, how to hunt, and how to build a den. They also learn how to avoid danger. The cubs' survival depends on learning these important lessons from their mother.

Grizzly cubs are very curious and playful. They spend much of their time exploring, tumbling in the grass, and playing with their cub mates. When their mother goes to sleep, the cubs often sleep on top of her. Grizzly mothers are very gentle and patient with their lively cubs, and they are fiercely protective.

Young grizzly cubs often have very dark brown fur with white patches on their necks or chests.

Guide to the Grizzly

At birth, a grizzly cub is about the size of a chipmunk.

Grizzly cubs learn everything they need to know about survival, including how to fish, by imitating their mother.

Development

Newborn grizzly cubs open their eyes and get their first teeth within a couple of weeks of birth. At this time, they also grow a coat of soft fur. The cubs grow quickly, gaining up to 8 pounds (3.6 kg) in their first months of life.

By the time cubs are 5 to 6 months old, they have become very active. As the weather gets warmer, they start to wander outside the den with their mother. Cubs continue to drink their mother's milk throughout this time. By 6 months, when they leave the den for good, they weigh as much as 30 pounds (14 kg).

The cubs continue to grow quickly. By the fall, they weigh anywhere from 50 to more than 100 pounds (23 to 45 kg). At this time, they are often **weaned**, although some bears will continue to nurse for several more months.

Most grizzly cubs remain with their mothers for about 2 years. Sometimes, however, cubs will stay with her for up to 4 years before going off on their own. A grizzly will not be ready to mate until it is about five years old.

Cubs are more vocal than adults. They will use different sounds to communicate with their mother and with other cubs.

Habitat

A grizzly bear needs a large area in which to live. Grizzlies can live in a variety of different habitats, including coastal areas, river valleys, grasslands, forests, and mountain meadows. Grizzlies eat such a wide variety of foods that they can live any place where there is enough space and enough food. In the United States, grizzly bears can be found in the area where southern Montana, western Idaho, and northwestern Wyoming border one another. Yellowstone National Park is in the middle of this region. Grizzly bears also live in an area of northwestern Montana that includes Glacier National Park. They are found as well in the Selkirk Mountains in western Montana and northern Idaho. In Canada, there are grizzly bears in the forests and mountains of Alberta and British Columbia. By far the greatest numbers of grizzly bears live in northern Canada and Alaska. The best grizzly habitat has very little human activity.

Organizing the Forest

Earth is home to millions of different **organisms**, all of which have specific survival needs. These organisms rely on their environment, or the place where they live, for their survival. All plants and animals have relationships with their environment. They interact with the environment itself, as well as the other plants and animals within the environment. These interactions create **ecosystems**.

Ecosystems can be broken down into levels of organization. These levels range from a single plant or animal to many species of plants and animals living together in an area.

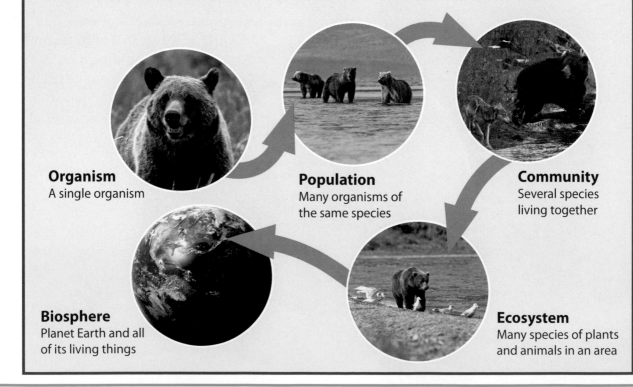

Organism
A single organism

Population
Many organisms of the same species

Community
Several species living together

Biosphere
Planet Earth and all of its living things

Ecosystem
Many species of plants and animals in an area

Guide to the Grizzly

Scientists can tell how old a grizzly is by looking at one of its teeth under a microscope. Grizzly teeth have rings, like tree rings, for every year of the bear's life.

The thick fur of the grizzly helps it survive in areas with very cold climates.

Home Range

Within a grizzly habitat, each bear has its own **home range**. An ideal home range is an area with both a great deal of food and good locations for dens. Male grizzly bears have larger home ranges than females. The home range of a female grizzly may be 100 square miles (260 square kilometers) or less, while the home range of a male grizzly may be as large as 1,500 square miles (3,900 sq. km).

The home range of one grizzly often overlaps with the ranges of other grizzlies. Grizzlies usually try to avoid one another, however. Adult male grizzlies will chase away any other male grizzlies who enter their home ranges.

In late spring, summer, and fall, grizzly bears often travel long distances in search of food. Throughout the day, grizzlies may stop to sleep on the ground or in a daybed. Grizzlies will dig several daybeds in their home ranges. These shallow holes are usually located near food sources, and they often have a good view of the surrounding area. Grizzlies will sometimes line their daybeds with leaves or pine needles.

A male grizzly will sniff the air or stand on its hind legs if it senses another bear in its home range.

In order to survive, grizzly bears sleep during the coldest months, when they are in their dens. Some people call this winter sleep **hibernation**. Many scientists, however, do not think that grizzlies truly hibernate. They call the grizzly bear's time in a den a winter dormant period.

During this period, the bear's whole body works more slowly to save energy. Normally, a grizzly bear breathes 6 to 10 times per minute. In the winter dormant period, a grizzly takes fewer than 2 breaths per minute. In addition, its heart slows from 70 beats per minute to only 8 to 10 beats per minute. While in their dens, grizzly bears do not eat, drink, or eliminate any waste. They survive by using the nutrients from their layers of fat. Grizzlies spend the entire winter in their dens.

Take a Stand
· Debate ·
· Research ·

Should grizzlies be kept in zoos?

Visitors can get close-up views of grizzly bears in zoos all over the world. These powerful animals are often one of a zoo's most popular attractions.

FOR

1. In most zoos, grizzlies are well fed and cared for. They are visited by **veterinarians** and have large areas in which to roam. Grizzlies in captivity usually live longer than grizzlies in nature.
2. When people have a chance to see grizzlies, they are more likely to care about these animals' future. Keeping grizzlies in zoos helps efforts to protect the bears and their habitats.

AGAINST

1. In nature, grizzlies are solitary animals with large home ranges. Even the largest zoos cannot give grizzlies a living area that is as good for the bears as their natural environment.
2. It is just not right to keep in captivity animals used to living in nature, even if zoos make efforts to provide good homes.

Diet

Grizzly bears are omnivores. This means that they eat both plants and animals. They can eat up to 35 pounds (16 kg) of food each day and almost three times that amount as they prepare to enter their winter dens. What a grizzly eats depends on where it lives and on the time of year. Grizzlies have excellent memories and can remember the locations of good food sources from one year to the next.

Grizzlies can hunt successfully during the day and at night, although they are usually most active during the day. Despite their enormous size, grizzly bears can run at speeds of up to 35 miles (55 km) per hour. Their strength, sharp teeth, and sharp claws make them very powerful hunters.

With their strong teeth and jaws, grizzlies are able to carry large prey. In general, they do not hunt large, healthy adult animals. Instead, they will often prey on sick or injured animals, as well as on newborn caribou, deer, or elk. Grizzlies will also feed on **carrion**.

Grizzlies use their sharp claws to dig up roots and insects. When looking for insect nests, the bears also use their claws to turn over rocks and logs. Grizzlies spend hours eating grasses, leaves, and seeds. They often eat sweet-tasting foods, such as berries and honey. The bears sometimes hunt small animals, such as mice and ground squirrels.

In regions where there are salmon in the rivers, grizzlies have different fishing methods. Some bears will sit on the edge of a river and grab salmon that pass by them. Others will stand on their four legs in the middle of a river and wait until fish swim into their paws and mouths.

Grizzlies that eat mostly plants are smaller than those with a great deal of fish in their diets.

Guide to the
Grizzly

Grizzlies will ignore the stings of angry bees just to get some honey from a beehive.

After catching a salmon, a grizzly will usually eat the eggs first.

The Food Cycle

A food cycle shows how energy in the form of food is passed from one living thing to another. As grizzly bears feed and move through their habitat, they affect the lives of the animals around them. The feeding habits of the grizzlies produce changes in the environment. In the diagram below, the arrows show the flow of energy from one living thing to the next through a **food web**.

Secondary Consumers
Very rarely, a **predator** such as a cougar will catch and eat a young or very old grizzly bear.

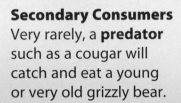

Primary Consumers
Grizzlies eat many types of plants, such as grasses, leaves, seeds, and berries.

Parasites
Grizzly bears provide a home for parasites such as the roundworm.

Omnivores
Besides plants, grizzlies also eat animals. These include salmon and squirrels.

Producers

Plants in forests and meadows produce food energy using sunlight. Grizzlies get food energy by eating these plants. Undigested seeds in grizzly droppings help new plants to grow. This ensures a continuing food supply for grizzlies and other animals.

Decomposers

When a grizzly dies, decomposers break down the bear's body materials, adding nutrients to the soil.

Take a Stand
Debate • Research

Should more land be set aside for grizzly bears?

In many places in North America, governments have set aside land for grizzly bears and other animals. In these areas, the bears' habitat is protected from development. Outside of protected areas, grizzlies are losing much of their habitat to new communities and farms. Bears are being driven from their home ranges into smaller areas of isolated wilderness.

FOR

1. Grizzly bears have large home ranges and need a great deal of space to find food. If more land is not set aside for grizzly habitat, the bears may not survive.
2. Grizzly bears share their habitats with many plants and other animals. If grizzly bears are protected, an environment in which many living things can thrive is being protected as well.

AGAINST

1. Humans cannot give up any more land, which is needed for development to meet people's needs. Grizzlies already have a great deal of open space in Alaska and northern Canada.
2. Farming is an important industry. If the land set aside for grizzlies is too close to farmland, the bears may attack livestock or eat crops. This will hurt farmers' incomes.

Guide to the
Grizzly

About half of all grizzly cubs do not live to adulthood.

Grizzlies will usually tolerate each other in places where there are a great many fish, but they may fight over the best fishing spots.

Competition

Grizzlies live in areas that have many different sources of food. Many other animals eat the same foods that grizzly bears eat, but there is usually enough food that competition is not necessary. By far the most dangerous competitors of grizzly bears are humans. In Canada and the United States, people are endangering the existence of the grizzly through poaching and by destroying the bears' habitats.

Competition between grizzlies is rare. Even though grizzlies sometimes look for food in the same area as other grizzlies, there is usually enough food to avoid competition. If a grizzly is using one food source, the other bear will just move on. Sometimes, fights occur between male grizzlies that are competing for the same female during the mating season. Male grizzlies will often kill bear cubs so they can mate with the mother. A female bear will not mate and have new cubs until her old cubs are gone. By killing bear cubs, a male grizzly can mate with the female much sooner.

Humans and grizzlies compete for territory. Growing human populations require land for homes, farms, industry, and recreation. As human activities move into grizzly territories, grizzlies are forced out. Grizzly bears survive best when they have little or no contact with humans. Grizzlies are sometimes shot because they are too close to homes, ranches, farms, or hiking areas. Since grizzlies often have only one or two cubs every three or four years, it takes a long time to replace grizzlies that have been taken by humans.

From an Expert

*"Alive, the grizzly is a symbol of freedom and understanding—a sign that man can conserve what is left of the earth. **Extinct**, it will be another fading testimony to things man should have learned more about, but was too preoccupied with himself to notice."* Frank Craighead

Frank Craighead was a naturalist and author. He and his identical twin, John, were considered some of the world's leading authorities on the grizzly bears in Yellowstone National Park. They were the first people to track large mammals with radio collars.

Grizzlies with Other Animals

As the biggest, strongest animal in its environment, the grizzly does not face much competition from other animals. If a grizzly is eating in one location, most other animals will avoid that area. Even wolves, aggressive hunters that travel in packs, will not often challenge a full-grown grizzly bear. Cubs are far more at risk than adult grizzly bears. If they get the chance, wolves or cougars will attack bear cubs. However, grizzly mothers are so careful and protective of their young that this does not happen often.

In many ways, the presence of grizzly bears helps the other animals in an environment. The presence of grizzlies is a sign that a natural environment is healthy. There must be many different types of food in an area if a grizzly is living there. If grizzly bears can find enough food, there is usually more than enough food for other animals.

The bears provide food for other animals when they leave partly eaten animal scraps. If there is a great deal of food available, grizzlies will sometimes eat just their favorite part. For example, they may eat just the fat and eggs of a salmon. The rest of the fish will be left for other animals to finish.

Grizzly bears may also help to prevent the spread of disease by eating dead or sick animals. The digestive systems of grizzly bears have adapted so that eating diseased or rotting animal flesh does not make the bears sick. Grizzlies also reduce the number of insects and rodents in an area.

Seagulls and other birds will feed on the leftovers of grizzly meals.

Grizzlies will tear apart rotting logs to look for insects to eat.

Grizzlies and wolves often live in the same areas. They usually avoid each other but are sometimes forced to compete if food is scarce.

Folklore

For centuries, bears have played a large part in the folklore of many cultures. Different cultures have stories about the resemblance between humans and a bear standing on its hind legs. Bears are often portrayed in folklore as smart, strong, and fair. Many stories describe grizzlies as mysterious. A few describe the bear as vicious and frightening. Many American Indian cultures consider the grizzly bear to be a sacred animal. Their stories often show admiration for the bear's powerful spirit.

Ancient Greeks and Romans thought the bear was very compassionate. Bears were often associated with nurses. This was probably because of the mother bear's well-known care and protection of her cubs. The ancient Greeks named two constellations, or groups of stars, after myths that are based on the bear. The Big Dipper forms the tail of Ursa Major, or the Great Bear. The Little Dipper forms Ursa Minor, or the Little Bear.

The grizzly bear is very important in many traditional American Indian stories. Many of these tales are about bears raising children and healing people. Medicine healers would use parts of the grizzly to treat illnesses. Grizzly bears were thought to have powerful spirits. After taking a grizzly, it was common for the hunters to apologize to the bear's spirit and have a ceremony to honor the bear. Some American Indians call the grizzly bear "grandfather" or "brother" out of respect.

In the 19th century, grizzly bears were often portrayed as vicious killers that would attack humans for no reason.

Myth	VS	Fact
Grizzlies attack people for no reason.		Grizzlies avoid humans. Grizzly attacks usually occur only when a grizzly feels threatened by a human or when a female grizzly believes her cubs are in danger.
Grizzlies are lazy and slow.		Grizzly bears often move slowly, as they eat or look for food in a part of their habitat. They can, however, run much more quickly than the fastest humans.
Grizzly bears cannot climb trees.		Although grizzly cubs climb trees in play or in times of danger, adult bears do not often climb trees. Grizzlies can, however, pull themselves up a tree just like humans can.

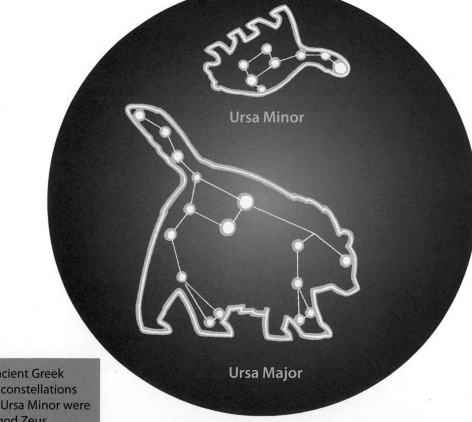

Ursa Minor

Ursa Major

According to ancient Greek mythology, the constellations Ursa Major and Ursa Minor were created by the god Zeus.

Grizzly bears once lived throughout the western half of North America, from Alaska to Mexico. The grizzly has since disappeared from most of its former habitat in the United States, except in Alaska. Although brown bears are quite common in other parts of the world, the grizzly subspecies is considered to be **threatened** in the United States, and it is **vulnerable** in Canada. This means the grizzly may be **endangered** if there is further legal hunting or poaching and habitat loss.

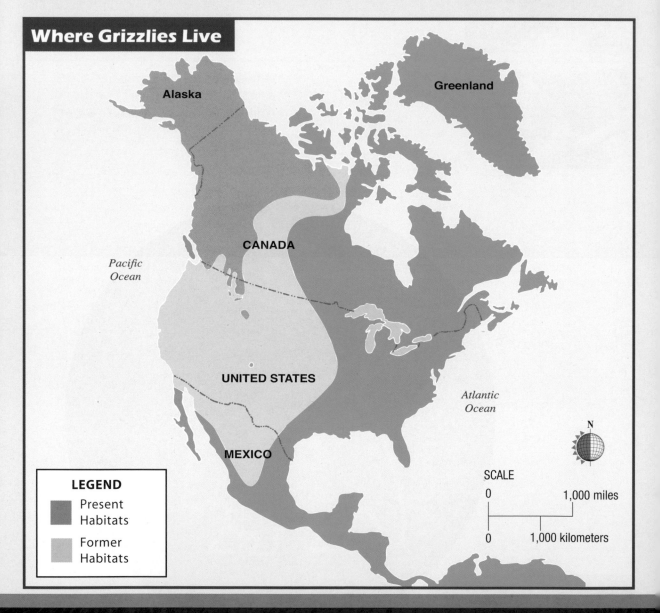

Where Grizzlies Live

Alaska

Greenland

CANADA

Pacific Ocean

UNITED STATES

Atlantic Ocean

MEXICO

N

SCALE

0   1,000 miles

0   1,000 kilometers

LEGEND

Present Habitats

Former Habitats

Where the hunting of grizzlies is allowed, governments are usually careful to limit the number of bears that can be taken each year. Bears are hunted for many reasons. Governments sometimes allow grizzly hunts if there are too many bears in one area. Hunters consider the grizzly to be a valuable prize because of its size and strength.

Sometimes, grizzlies are taken by people who are hunting for sport but who do not have a hunting license. Many times, illegal hunting is done for profit. Grizzly bear parts are sometimes made into trophies for display, including mounted bear heads, hides, or paws. Sometimes, grizzly parts are made into jewelry or ashtrays. Many people around the world will pay a great deal of money for these items. Some people believe that they become stronger if they own a piece of such a powerful animal. In certain cultures, some grizzly bear body parts, such as the gallbladder and the paws, are believed to have magical powers and are used in medicines. Poachers often take grizzly bears so they can make money selling these body parts.

Habitat loss is the greatest threat to grizzly bears. Grizzlies once lived on the Great Plains. In the 19th and 20th centuries, most of these bears were hunted by humans. People shot the bears out of fear, for food, for sport, or because they interfered with land settlement. Today, as human populations continue to move into grizzly territory, the bears are forced into areas that do not have enough food or into spaces that bring them in more contact with humans.

• Debate •
Take a Stand
• Research •

Should grizzly bears be removed from the U.S. government's list of threatened animals?

In 1975, under the Endangered Species Act, the grizzly bear was listed as a threatened animal in the United States, except for Alaska and Hawai'i. Grizzlies have never lived in Hawai'i.

FOR

1. Grizzly bears are one of the few protected animals that may attack humans, though they rarely do so. People are afraid to live in areas where bear populations have increased but hunting is not allowed.
2. Grizzlies may eat livestock. Ranchers should be allowed to shoot bears if their animals are in danger. Shooting a threatened or endangered animal is often illegal unless a human life is in danger.

AGAINST

1. Grizzly attacks on humans are rare, often fewer than five per year. They can usually be prevented by taking precautions to avoid surprising the bears. Precautions such as electrified fences can help prevent bear attacks on farm animals.
2. Removing the protection grizzly bears have as a threatened animal would undo the progress that has been made. Many scientists believe the grizzly population must increase much more before this bear is truly safe from the risk of extinction.

Guide to the Grizzly

Grizzly bears will eat food scraps in garbage if they can get this food with little effort. They will return again and again to unprotected garbage dumps.

People must be very careful about storing food and garbage in areas where grizzlies live. Camping grounds often provide places to hang food above a grizzly's reach.

Saving the Grizzly Bear

Many steps have been taken to prevent the grizzly bear from disappearing in the United States and in Canada. In North America, it is illegal to buy or sell the parts of a protected animal without a special license. In spite of these laws, poachers still take some grizzly bears and sell their body parts.

To protect grizzlies, it is important to protect the land in which they live. Grizzly bear reserves have been set up in many national, state, and provincial parks in North America. In these areas, human activity is limited, so that the bears' habitats can be preserved.

One of the biggest dangers to the grizzly occurs when bears become used to the presence of humans and to human food and garbage as a food source. These bears often have to be shot because they become a danger to humans. National and provincial parks and campgrounds have very strict rules about how and where people should store their food and dispose of their trash. There are also rules for human visitors about how to enjoy wilderness areas without damaging them. These rules help to protect both bears and humans. Despite all of these efforts, many people think the grizzly may soon exist only in Alaska and northern Canada.

From an Expert

"The grizzly will survive as long as there is a place for him and as long as man lets him survive. . . . Ultimately, you and I have the final say on the continued existence of this great animal, the grizzly."
Alan Carey

Alan Carey is a professional wildlife photographer and researcher who has long been fascinated by grizzly bears. He is author of the book *In the Path of the Grizzly*.

Back from the Brink

One of the best places to see grizzly bears in nature is at the McNeil River State Wildlife Sanctuary in Alaska. The sanctuary is home to the world's largest known population of grizzly bears. At the McNeil waterfalls, visitors have seen up to 75 bears at a time, all fishing for salmon. Human activity is kept to a minimum in the sanctuary. The number of visitors is strictly limited. Land development, hunting, and trapping are not allowed. Great care is taken to see that humans do not disturb the bears. Since the sanctuary was created, there have been no bear attacks on people. No bear has needed to be destroyed.

To see the bears, people must first enter a lottery. Only the few lottery winners are allowed into the reserve each year. Bear experts are available to answer visitors' questions. For more information on the McNeil River State Wildlife Sanctuary and how to enter the lottery, contact:

Alaska Department of Fish and Game
Division of Wildlife Conservation
P.O. Box 228080
Attention: 2014 McNeil River Application
Anchorage, Alaska 99522-8080

At the McNeil River State Wildlife Sanctuary in Alaska, grizzlies can fish for five different species of salmon. Visitors must follow strict rules to keep from disturbing the bears.

Activity

Debating helps people think about ideas thoughtfully and carefully. When people debate, two sides take a different viewpoint on a subject. Each side takes turns presenting arguments to support its view.

Use the Take a Stand sections found throughout this book as a starting point for debate topics. Organize your friends or classmates into two teams. One team will argue in favor of the topic, and the other will argue against. Each team should research the issue thoroughly using reliable sources of information, including books, scientific journals, and trustworthy websites. Take notes of important facts that support your side of the debate. Prepare your argument using these facts to support your opinion.

During the debate, the members of each team are given a set amount of time to make their arguments. The team arguing the For side goes first. They have five minutes to present their case. All members of the team should participate equally. Then, the team arguing the Against side presents its arguments. Each team should take notes of the main points the other team argues.

After both teams have made their arguments, they get three minutes to prepare their rebuttals. Teams review their notes from the previous round. The teams focus on trying to disprove each of the main points made by the other team using solid facts. Each team gets three minutes to make its rebuttal. The team arguing the Against side goes first. Students and teachers watching the debate serve as judges. They should try to judge the debate fairly using a standard score sheet, such as the example below.

Criteria	Rate: 1-10	Sample Comments
1. Were the arguments well organized?	8	logical arguments, easy to follow
2. Did team members participate equally?	9	divided time evenly between members
3. Did team members speak loudly and clearly?	3	some members were difficult to hear
4. Were rebuttals specific to the other team's arguments?	6	rebuttals were specific, more facts needed
5. Was respect shown for the other team?	10	all members showed respect to the other team

2. How many teeth does a grizzly bear have?

3. About how long is the gestation period for grizzlies?

1. What is the top speed of a grizzly bear?

5. Where is the world's largest known population of grizzly bears?

4. True or false: Grizzly cubs have no teeth at birth.

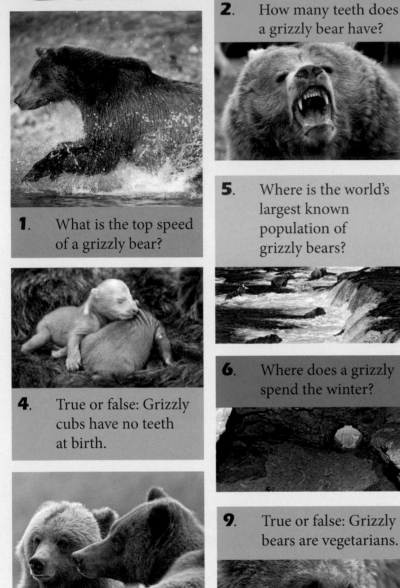

6. Where does a grizzly spend the winter?

7. What are the two main things a grizzly needs in its home range?

9. True or false: Grizzly bears are vegetarians.

10. How many cubs does a mother grizzly usually have at one time?

8. At about what age is a grizzly ready to mate?

Answers:
1. 35 miles (55 km) per hour 2. 42 3. 3 months 4. true 5. McNeil River State Wildlife Sanctuary in Alaska 6. in a den 7. food and good locations for dens 8. 5 years old 9. false 10. two

Key Words

adaptations: changes made to fit into a certain environment

camouflage: when an animal's appearance blends in with its environment, so that the animal is very hard to see

carnivores: animals that eat meat

carrion: the flesh of a dead animal

ecosystems: communities of living things and resources

endangered: at risk of no longer surviving in the world

extinct: no longer surviving in the world

food web: connecting food chains that show how energy flows from one organism to another through diet

gestation period: the length of time that a female is pregnant

grizzled: sprinkled or streaked with white or gray

guard hairs: the long, straight, coarse hairs that lie over the underfur of an animal

habitat: the place where an animal lives, grows, and raises its young

hibernation: a period of time during the winter when certain animals' body temperature and heart rate drop a great deal to save energy

home range: the entire area in which a grizzly bear lives

order: one of eight major ranks used to classify animals, between class and family

organisms: forms of life

poaching: killing an animal illegally

predator: an animal that lives by hunting other animals for food

species: groups of individuals with common characteristics

threatened: at risk of becoming endangered

veterinarians: doctors who care for animals

vulnerable: at risk of becoming threatened or endangered if not protected

weaned: when a young animal does not drink milk from its mother anymore

Index

Log on to www.av2books.com

AV² by Weigl brings you media enhanced books that support active learning. Go to www.av2books.com, and enter the special code found on page 2 of this book. You will gain access to enriched and enhanced content that supplements and complements this book. Content includes video, audio, weblinks, quizzes, a slide show, and activities.

AV² Online Navigation

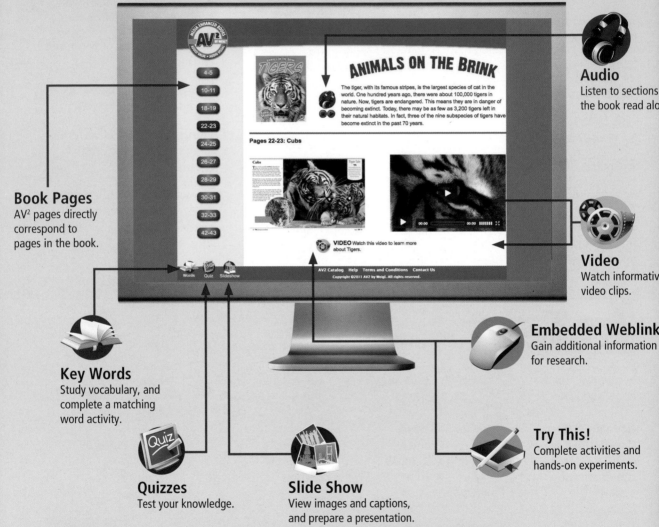

Audio
Listen to sections the book read alo

Book Pages
AV² pages directly correspond to pages in the book.

Video
Watch informativ video clips.

Embedded Weblink
Gain additional information for research.

Key Words
Study vocabulary, and complete a matching word activity.

Try This!
Complete activities and hands-on experiments.

Quizzes
Test your knowledge.

Slide Show
View images and captions, and prepare a presentation.

AV² was built to bridge the gap between print and digital. We encourage you to tell us what you like and what you want to see in the future.

Sign up to be an AV² Ambassador at www.av2books.com/ambassador.

Due to the dynamic nature of the Internet, some of the URLs and activities provided as part of AV² by Weigl may have changed or ceased to exist. AV² by Weigl accepts no responsibility for any such changes. All media enhanced books are regularly monitored to update addresses and sites in a timely manner. Contact AV² by Weigl at 1-866-649-3445 or av2books@weigl.com with any questions, comments, or feedback.